The

5 Minute Journal

"If we change the way we look at things, the things we look at change"

☀ MON 4/10/21

Today I am expressing gratitude for
- The view from our hotel bungalow in Athens
- Uday being so supportive through this flare up.
- My life — I am truly blessed

Three mini goals for making today great
- Some gentle movement, perhaps a swim
- Thanking Uday for what he does for me
- Appreciating the ocean beauty in front of me.

My Todays Affirmations, I am
- Strong
- Grateful

Three things that happened today for which I am grateful
- I managed to exercise a little in the pool.
- I managed to walk a total of 3.5 km without too much pain.
- I only had a tiny bowel leak (could have been a size

How I might have advanced the quality of my day
- I tried very hard to not give in to the pain today
- I worked on appreciating the now

"Live life as if everything is rigged in your favor"

5/10/21

Today I am expressing gratitude for

- My birth, this life, this earth
- My resilience
- My husband

Three mini goals for making today great

- Take in and appreciate your surroundings
- Tell people your truth right now
- Love yourself

My Todays Affirmations, I am

- Worthy
- Resilient

Three things that happened today for which I am grateful

- Lots of birthday calls & messages
- Spending time with Uday and alone
- The glorious weather and scenery here at the Astir Palace

How I might have advanced the quality of my day

- Being honest about how I feel
- Slowing down and accepting my current pace.

"Life does not happen to me; it happens for me"

☀ WED 6/10/21

Today I am expressing gratitude for

- Sleep, when it finally came
- Being alive
- So many friendships I find hard to acknowledge

Three mini goals for making today great

- Staying in the now
- Taking it slow
- Seeing the beauty in what Surrounds me.

My Todays Affirmations, I am

- Strong
- Healthy

🌙

Three things that happened today for which I am grateful

- I walked 4km around the resort
- I had a lovely afternoon nap
- Nice dinner w. Ed Rom & his wife Mel

How I might have advanced the quality of my day

- Spending more time appreciating the scenery
- Trying to move more

"If you don't like how things are change them, you are not a tree"

☀ Thu 7/10/21

Today I am expressing gratitude for

- A good nights sleep
- Companionship, Uday being in my life
- Nature, the view, the sounds, the smells, All of it!

Three mini goals for making today great

- Keep moving
- Smile more
- Express the positives, even the small ones

My Todays Affirmations, I am

- Happy
- Healthy

🌙

Three things that happened today for which I am grateful

- It was warmer, summer, less windy
- 1 hr Navrati chant/meditation
- Wonderful, delicious dinner

How I might have advanced the quality of my day

- Smiling more makes things better ✓
- Did my exercises - pool, kegel, walk

> *"People with goals succeed because they know the direction they are headed"*

FRI 8/10/21

Today I am expressing gratitude for

- Sleep, rest and being allowed to slow down
- Uday being a part of my life
- My improving health

Three mini goals for making today great

- More smiles
- Meditation
-

My Todays Affirmations, I am

- Strong
- Kind

Three things that happened today for which I am grateful

- The slowest of days to remind me that too slow is also not what I want
- Lots of time for meditations
- Fantastic spa treatment

How I might have advanced the quality of my day

- I smiled
- I set boundaries and did what I wanted to do.

"The bridge between goals and accomplishment is discipline"

Sat 9/10/21

Today I am expressing gratitude for

- Having time to rest and heal
- My sexuality, that it's still active
- My family, Uday & the children

Three mini goals for making today great

- Smile
- Stay calm
- Enjoy!

My Todays Affirmations, I am

- Healthy
- Happy

Three things that happened today for which I am grateful

-
-
-

How I might have advanced the quality of my day

-
-

"Our attitude towards others determines their attitude towards us"

☀ Sun 10/10/21

Today I am expressing gratitude for

- My health
- My financial situation /not having to work
- Peace and quiet

Three mini goals for making today great

- Long bath
- No rush - do what you want when you want
- Time to myself - prioritise it

My Todays Affirmations, I am

- Worthy
- Enough

Three things that happened today for which I am grateful

- Nothing happened today
- I spent the day colouring in
- patterns and listening to an audiobook.

How I might have advanced the quality of my day

- I could have gone for a walk
- I could have gone for a swim

"Creativity is the natural extension of our enthusiasm"

MON 11/10/21

Today I am expressing gratitude for

- My resilience - it is there even after days like yesterday.
- ~~A NEW DAY~~
- The silence of the morning

Three mini goals for making today great

- Try not to cry
- Enjoy the OHCF lunch
- Cook a healthy and tasty dinner

My Todays Affirmations, I am

- Strong
- Healthy

Three things that happened today for which I am grateful

- The afternoon passed quickly
- Hiral's call
- The sun shone for a bit. Lovely

How I might have advanced the quality of my day

- Be less fearful of what the future may bring
- Gone for a walk. Use the dog!

"Work never killed anyone it's the worry that does the damage and the worry disappears when we work"

TUE OCT 12TH 2021

Today I am expressing gratitude for

- Seeing the sun rise this morning
- The quiet of my room
- The feeling of air in my nostrils as I inhale

Three mini goals for making today great

- Smile
- Listen
- Walk away if you need to

My Todays Affirmations, I am

- Me
- Peace

Three things that happened today for which I am grateful

- I left the CBUK lunch early.
- Didn't feel guilty about it!
- My therapy session w. Peter. Just grateful he's there

How I might have advanced the quality of my day

- Said No to the lunch
- Afternoon bath. ~~With the one hour~~ !

"What we plant in our subconscious mind and nourish with emotion and repetition becomes our reality"

WED OCT 13TH 2021

Today I am expressing gratitude for
- Nerva App. Hypnosis for IBS
- Kieran Macphail - my physio
- A new day

Three mini goals for making today great
- Trust in your body's healing ability
- Remember that change is inevitable
- Smile

My Todays Affirmations, I am
- Strong
- Patient

She didn't pick up

Three things that happened today for which I am grateful
- I rested instead of meeting Sheena
- Zahida called and I laughed
- Uday is back home safely

Keefan answered my text. Seems ok.

How I might have advanced the quality of my day
- By walking to the vet?
- By swimming in the afternoon?

"Life is 10% what happens to you and 90% how you react to it"

☀ Thu Oct 14TH 2021

Today I am expressing gratitude for
- Watching the Sunrise from my window
- Feeling the Sun on my face
- A new day

Three mini goals for making today great
- Exercise
- Smile
- Compile a to do list - cross one thing off

My Todays Affirmations, I am
- Happy
- Strong

Three things that happened today for which I am grateful
-
-
-

How I might have advanced the quality of my day
-
-

"I control how I feel"

Today I am expressing gratitude for

- _____
- _____
- _____

Three mini goals for making today great

- _____
- _____
- _____

My Todays Affirmations, I am

- _____
- _____

Three things that happened today for which I am grateful

- _____
- _____
- _____

How I might have advanced the quality of my day

- _____
- _____

"For every disciplined effort there are multiple rewards"

Today I am expressing gratitude for

- _____
- _____
- _____

Three mini goals for making today great

- _____
- _____
- _____

My Todays Affirmations, I am

- _____
- _____

Three things that happened today for which I am grateful

- _____
- _____
- _____

How I might have advanced the quality of my day

- _____
- _____

"Whatever the mind can conceive and believe it can achieve"

Today I am expressing gratitude for

- _____
- _____
- _____

Three mini goals for making today great

- _____
- _____
- _____

My Todays Affirmations, I am

- _____
- _____

Three things that happened today for which I am grateful

- _____
- _____
- _____

How I might have advanced the quality of my day

- _____
- _____

"Your outer foundation comes from your inner strength"

Today I am expressing gratitude for

- _____
- _____
- _____

Three mini goals for making today great

- _____
- _____
- _____

My Todays Affirmations, I am

- _____
- _____

Three things that happened today for which I am grateful

- _____
- _____
- _____

How I might have advanced the quality of my day

- _____
- _____

"Your income seldom exceeds personal development, so invest in yourself"

Today I am expressing gratitude for

- _____
- _____
- _____

Three mini goals for making today great

- _____
- _____
- _____

My Todays Affirmations, I am

- _____
- _____

Three things that happened today for which I am grateful

- _____
- _____
- _____

How I might have advanced the quality of my day

- _____
- _____

"Life is constantly happening to make me happy and successful"

Today I am expressing gratitude for

- _____
- _____
- _____

Three mini goals for making today great

- _____
- _____
- _____

My Todays Affirmations, I am

- _____
- _____

Three things that happened today for which I am grateful

- _____
- _____
- _____

How I might have advanced the quality of my day

- _____
- _____

"If you want to become rich yourself enrich others"

Today I am expressing gratitude for

- _____
- _____
- _____

Three mini goals for making today great

- _____
- _____
- _____

My Todays Affirmations, I am

- _____
- _____

Three things that happened today for which I am grateful

- _____
- _____
- _____

How I might have advanced the quality of my day

- _____
- _____

"If you cannot dream yourself into a character you must hammer and forge yourself one"

Today I am expressing gratitude for

- _____
- _____
- _____

Three mini goals for making today great

- _____
- _____
- _____

My Todays Affirmations, I am

- _____
- _____

Three things that happened today for which I am grateful

- _____
- _____
- _____

How I might have advanced the quality of my day

- _____
- _____

"Happiness is not something which you postpone, express gratitude and be happy in the moment"

Today I am expressing gratitude for

- _____
- _____
- _____

Three mini goals for making today great

- _____
- _____
- _____

My Todays Affirmations, I am

- _____
- _____

Three things that happened today for which I am grateful

- _____
- _____
- _____

How I might have advanced the quality of my day

- _____
- _____

"I will improve 1% each day and give myself the pleasure for tiny progress"

Today I am expressing gratitude for

- _____
- _____
- _____

Three mini goals for making today great

- _____
- _____
- _____

My Todays Affirmations, I am

- _____
- _____

Three things that happened today for which I am grateful

- _____
- _____
- _____

How I might have advanced the quality of my day

- _____
- _____

"Success is simple disciplines practiced everyday"

Today I am expressing gratitude for

- _____
- _____
- _____

Three mini goals for making today great

- _____
- _____
- _____

My Todays Affirmations, I am

- _____
- _____

Three things that happened today for which I am grateful

- _____
- _____
- _____

How I might have advanced the quality of my day

- _____
- _____

"I'm at the level now where I'm done talking, it's just time to execute."

Today I am expressing gratitude for

- _____
- _____
- _____

Three mini goals for making today great

- _____
- _____
- _____

My Todays Affirmations, I am

- _____
- _____

Three things that happened today for which I am grateful

- _____
- _____
- _____

How I might have advanced the quality of my day

- _____
- _____

"The only person you are destined to become is the person you decide to be"

Today I am expressing gratitude for

- _____
- _____
- _____

Three mini goals for making today great

- _____
- _____
- _____

My Todays Affirmations, I am

- _____
- _____

Three things that happened today for which I am grateful

- _____
- _____
- _____

How I might have advanced the quality of my day

- _____
- _____

"If you are not willing to risk the unusual, you will always have to settle for the ordinary"

Today I am expressing gratitude for

- _____
- _____
- _____

Three mini goals for making today great

- _____
- _____
- _____

My Todays Affirmations, I am

- _____
- _____

Three things that happened today for which I am grateful

- _____
- _____
- _____

How I might have advanced the quality of my day

- _____
- _____

"Overnight you cannot change your destination, but you can change your direction"

Today I am expressing gratitude for

- _____
- _____
- _____

Three mini goals for making today great

- _____
- _____
- _____

My Todays Affirmations, I am

- _____
- _____

Three things that happened today for which I am grateful

- _____
- _____
- _____

How I might have advanced the quality of my day

- _____
- _____

"True nobility is being superior to your former self"

Today I am expressing gratitude for

- _____
- _____
- _____

Three mini goals for making today great

- _____
- _____
- _____

My Todays Affirmations, I am

- _____
- _____

Three things that happened today for which I am grateful

- _____
- _____
- _____

How I might have advanced the quality of my day

- _____
- _____

"Secret to success is staying committed to your decisions but staying flexible in your approach"

Today I am expressing gratitude for

- _____
- _____
- _____

Three mini goals for making today great

- _____
- _____
- _____

My Todays Affirmations, I am

- _____
- _____

Three things that happened today for which I am grateful

- _____
- _____
- _____

How I might have advanced the quality of my day

- _____
- _____

"Work harder on yourself than you do on your Job"

Today I am expressing gratitude for

- _____
- _____
- _____

Three mini goals for making today great

- _____
- _____
- _____

My Todays Affirmations, I am

- _____
- _____

Three things that happened today for which I am grateful

- _____
- _____
- _____

How I might have advanced the quality of my day

- _____
- _____

"In this world you are either growing or dying, so get in motion and grow"

Today I am expressing gratitude for

- _____
- _____
- _____

Three mini goals for making today great

- _____
- _____
- _____

My Todays Affirmations, I am

- _____
- _____

Three things that happened today for which I am grateful

- _____
- _____
- _____

How I might have advanced the quality of my day

- _____
- _____

"If you want different fruits you will first have to change the roots"

Today I am expressing gratitude for

- _____
- _____
- _____

Three mini goals for making today great

- _____
- _____
- _____

My Todays Affirmations, I am

- _____
- _____

Three things that happened today for which I am grateful

- _____
- _____
- _____

How I might have advanced the quality of my day

- _____
- _____

"Mind acts like a muscle, the more you use it the stronger it becomes"

Today I am expressing gratitude for

- _____
- _____
- _____

Three mini goals for making today great

- _____
- _____
- _____

My Todays Affirmations, I am

- _____
- _____

Three things that happened today for which I am grateful

- _____
- _____
- _____

How I might have advanced the quality of my day

- _____
- _____

"Desire loses it's value without a sense of urgency"

Today I am expressing gratitude for

- _____
- _____
- _____

Three mini goals for making today great

- _____
- _____
- _____

My Todays Affirmations, I am

- _____
- _____

Three things that happened today for which I am grateful

- _____
- _____
- _____

How I might have advanced the quality of my day

- _____
- _____

"Success is achieved when we do ordinary things extraordinarily well"

Today I am expressing gratitude for

- _____
- _____
- _____

Three mini goals for making today great

- _____
- _____
- _____

My Todays Affirmations, I am

- _____
- _____

Three things that happened today for which I am grateful

- _____
- _____
- _____

How I might have advanced the quality of my day

- _____
- _____

"We become what we think about most of the time"

Today I am expressing gratitude for

- _____
- _____
- _____

Three mini goals for making today great

- _____
- _____
- _____

My Todays Affirmations, I am

- _____
- _____

Three things that happened today for which I am grateful

- _____
- _____
- _____

How I might have advanced the quality of my day

- _____
- _____

*"If you want to lead an extraordinary life, find out
what the ordinary do and don't do that"*

Today I am expressing gratitude for

- _____

- _____

- _____

Three mini goals for making today great

- _____

- _____

- _____

My Todays Affirmations, I am

- _____

- _____

Three things that happened today for which I am grateful

- _____

- _____

- _____

How I might have advanced the quality of my day

- _____

- _____

"Miss a meal if you have to but don't miss reading"

Today I am expressing gratitude for

- _____
- _____
- _____

Three mini goals for making today great

- _____
- _____
- _____

My Todays Affirmations, I am

- _____
- _____

Three things that happened today for which I am grateful

- _____
- _____
- _____

How I might have advanced the quality of my day

- _____
- _____

"Success is something not to be pursued but to be attracted by the person you become"

Today I am expressing gratitude for

- _____
- _____
- _____

Three mini goals for making today great

- _____
- _____
- _____

My Todays Affirmations, I am

- _____
- _____

Three things that happened today for which I am grateful

- _____
- _____
- _____

How I might have advanced the quality of my day

- _____
- _____

"Your destiny is shaped in the moments of decisions"

Today I am expressing gratitude for

- _____
- _____
- _____

Three mini goals for making today great

- _____
- _____
- _____

My Todays Affirmations, I am

- _____
- _____

Three things that happened today for which I am grateful

- _____
- _____
- _____

How I might have advanced the quality of my day

- _____
- _____

"The path to success is filled with taking massive determined action"

Today I am expressing gratitude for

- _____
- _____
- _____

Three mini goals for making today great

- _____
- _____
- _____

My Todays Affirmations, I am

- _____
- _____

Three things that happened today for which I am grateful

- _____
- _____
- _____

How I might have advanced the quality of my day

- _____
- _____

"The only limit to your success in life is your imagination and your commitment"

Today I am expressing gratitude for

- _____
- _____
- _____

Three mini goals for making today great

- _____
- _____
- _____

My Todays Affirmations, I am

- _____
- _____

Three things that happened today for which I am grateful

- _____
- _____
- _____

How I might have advanced the quality of my day

- _____
- _____

"Successful people ask better questions and as a result they get better answers"

Today I am expressing gratitude for

- _____
- _____
- _____

Three mini goals for making today great

- _____
- _____
- _____

My Todays Affirmations, I am

- _____
- _____

Three things that happened today for which I am grateful

- _____
- _____
- _____

How I might have advanced the quality of my day

- _____
- _____

"In order to get more you must become more"

Today I am expressing gratitude for

- _____
- _____
- _____

Three mini goals for making today great

- _____
- _____
- _____

My Todays Affirmations, I am

- _____
- _____

Three things that happened today for which I am grateful

- _____
- _____
- _____

How I might have advanced the quality of my day

- _____
- _____

"Failure does not exist there are only results"

Today I am expressing gratitude for

- _____
- _____
- _____

Three mini goals for making today great

- _____
- _____
- _____

My Todays Affirmations, I am

- _____
- _____

Three things that happened today for which I am grateful

- _____
- _____
- _____

How I might have advanced the quality of my day

- _____
- _____

"Successful people have one thing in common, an absolute sense of clarity"

Today I am expressing gratitude for

- _____
- _____
- _____

Three mini goals for making today great

- _____
- _____
- _____

My Todays Affirmations, I am

- _____
- _____

Three things that happened today for which I am grateful

- _____
- _____
- _____

How I might have advanced the quality of my day

- _____
- _____

"If you are committed there is always a way"

Today I am expressing gratitude for

- _____
- _____
- _____

Three mini goals for making today great

- _____
- _____
- _____

My Todays Affirmations, I am

- _____
- _____

Three things that happened today for which I am grateful

- _____
- _____
- _____

How I might have advanced the quality of my day

- _____
- _____

"As long as you do not stop, it does not matter how slowly you go"

Today I am expressing gratitude for

- _____
- _____
- _____

Three mini goals for making today great

- _____
- _____
- _____

My Todays Affirmations, I am

- _____
- _____

Three things that happened today for which I am grateful

- _____
- _____
- _____

How I might have advanced the quality of my day

- _____
- _____

"Repetition is the mother of Mastery"

Today I am expressing gratitude for

- _____
- _____
- _____

Three mini goals for making today great

- _____
- _____
- _____

My Todays Affirmations, I am

- _____
- _____

Three things that happened today for which I am grateful

- _____
- _____
- _____

How I might have advanced the quality of my day

- _____
- _____

"Where focus goes energy flows"

Today I am expressing gratitude for

- _____
- _____
- _____

Three mini goals for making today great

- _____
- _____
- _____

My Todays Affirmations, I am

- _____
- _____

Three things that happened today for which I am grateful

- _____
- _____
- _____

How I might have advanced the quality of my day

- _____
- _____

"Your past does not equal to your future"

Today I am expressing gratitude for

- _____
- _____
- _____

Three mini goals for making today great

- _____
- _____
- _____

My Todays Affirmations, I am

- _____
- _____

Three things that happened today for which I am grateful

- _____
- _____
- _____

How I might have advanced the quality of my day

- _____
- _____

"When universe hands you a lemon make a lemonade."

Today I am expressing gratitude for

- _____
- _____
- _____

Three mini goals for making today great

- _____
- _____
- _____

My Todays Affirmations, I am

- _____
- _____

Three things that happened today for which I am grateful

- _____
- _____
- _____

How I might have advanced the quality of my day

- _____
- _____

"What seems to us as bitter trials are often blessings in disguise"

Today I am expressing gratitude for

- _____
- _____
- _____

Three mini goals for making today great

- _____
- _____
- _____

My Todays Affirmations, I am

- _____
- _____

Three things that happened today for which I am grateful

- _____
- _____
- _____

How I might have advanced the quality of my day

- _____
- _____

"I'm at the level now where I'm done talking, it's just time to execute."

Today I am expressing gratitude for

- _____
- _____
- _____

Three mini goals for making today great

- _____
- _____
- _____

My Todays Affirmations, I am

- _____
- _____

Three things that happened today for which I am grateful

- _____
- _____
- _____

How I might have advanced the quality of my day

- _____
- _____

"No one can make me feel inferior without my permission"

Today I am expressing gratitude for

- _____
- _____
- _____

Three mini goals for making today great

- _____
- _____
- _____

My Todays Affirmations, I am

- _____
- _____

Three things that happened today for which I am grateful

- _____
- _____
- _____

How I might have advanced the quality of my day

- _____
- _____

"In our moments of decision, our destiny is shaped "

Today I am expressing gratitude for

- _____
- _____
- _____

Three mini goals for making today great

- _____
- _____
- _____

My Todays Affirmations, I am

- _____
- _____

Three things that happened today for which I am grateful

- _____
- _____
- _____

How I might have advanced the quality of my day

- _____
- _____

"Foundation of abundance in life is acknowledging the good, you already have"

Today I am expressing gratitude for

- _____
- _____
- _____

Three mini goals for making today great

- _____
- _____
- _____

My Todays Affirmations, I am

- _____
- _____

Three things that happened today for which I am grateful

- _____
- _____
- _____

How I might have advanced the quality of my day

- _____
- _____

"Imagination and commitment are the only limitations, to the impact you will have on this world"

Today I am expressing gratitude for

- _____
- _____
- _____

Three mini goals for making today great

- _____
- _____
- _____

My Todays Affirmations, I am

- _____
- _____

Three things that happened today for which I am grateful

- _____
- _____
- _____

How I might have advanced the quality of my day

- _____
- _____

"Your goals should excite you a lot and scare you a little"

Today I am expressing gratitude for

- _____
- _____
- _____

Three mini goals for making today great

- _____
- _____
- _____

My Todays Affirmations, I am

- _____
- _____

Three things that happened today for which I am grateful

- _____
- _____
- _____

How I might have advanced the quality of my day

- _____
- _____

"Your thoughts and beliefs create your reality but only when you are happy in your present, so stop postponing happiness"

Today I am expressing gratitude for

- _____
- _____
- _____

Three mini goals for making today great

- _____
- _____
- _____

My Todays Affirmations, I am

- _____
- _____

Three things that happened today for which I am grateful

- _____
- _____
- _____

How I might have advanced the quality of my day

- _____
- _____

"People often say that motivation doesn't last. Well, neither does bathing - that's why we recommend it daily."

Today I am expressing gratitude for

- _____
- _____
- _____

Three mini goals for making today great

- _____
- _____
- _____

My Todays Affirmations, I am

- _____
- _____

Three things that happened today for which I am grateful

- _____
- _____
- _____

How I might have advanced the quality of my day

- _____
- _____

"The genesis of genius is passion"

Today I am expressing gratitude for

- _____
- _____
- _____

Three mini goals for making today great

- _____
- _____
- _____

My Todays Affirmations, I am

- _____
- _____

Three things that happened today for which I am grateful

- _____
- _____
- _____

How I might have advanced the quality of my day

- _____
- _____

"Events don't shape our lives but the meaning we attach to them does"

Today I am expressing gratitude for

- _____
- _____
- _____

Three mini goals for making today great

- _____
- _____
- _____

My Todays Affirmations, I am

- _____
- _____

Three things that happened today for which I am grateful

- _____
- _____
- _____

How I might have advanced the quality of my day

- _____
- _____

"The gift of unconditional love and acceptance is the greatest gift you can give to others"

Today I am expressing gratitude for

- _____
- _____
- _____

Three mini goals for making today great

- _____
- _____
- _____

My Todays Affirmations, I am

- _____
- _____

Three things that happened today for which I am grateful

- _____
- _____
- _____

How I might have advanced the quality of my day

- _____
- _____

"Successful people are always looking for opportunities to help others"

Today I am expressing gratitude for

- _____
- _____
- _____

Three mini goals for making today great

- _____
- _____
- _____

My Todays Affirmations, I am

- _____
- _____

Three things that happened today for which I am grateful

- _____
- _____
- _____

How I might have advanced the quality of my day

- _____
- _____

"The key to success is to focus your conscious mind on things you desire and not the things you fear"

Today I am expressing gratitude for

- _____
- _____
- _____

Three mini goals for making today great

- _____
- _____
- _____

My Todays Affirmations, I am

- _____
- _____

Three things that happened today for which I am grateful

- _____
- _____
- _____

How I might have advanced the quality of my day

- _____
- _____

"Have audacious goals but don't tie your happiness to them be happy in the now"

Today I am expressing gratitude for

- _____
- _____
- _____

Three mini goals for making today great

- _____
- _____
- _____

My Todays Affirmations, I am

- _____
- _____

Three things that happened today for which I am grateful

- _____
- _____
- _____

How I might have advanced the quality of my day

- _____
- _____

"The best revenge is massive success"

Today I am expressing gratitude for

- _____
- _____
- _____

Three mini goals for making today great

- _____
- _____
- _____

My Todays Affirmations, I am

- _____
- _____

Three things that happened today for which I am grateful

- _____
- _____
- _____

How I might have advanced the quality of my day

- _____
- _____

"I speak my dreams into reality"

Today I am expressing gratitude for

- _____
- _____
- _____

Three mini goals for making today great

- _____
- _____
- _____

My Todays Affirmations, I am

- _____
- _____

Three things that happened today for which I am grateful

- _____
- _____
- _____

How I might have advanced the quality of my day

- _____
- _____

"I live in the bliss of discipline"

Today I am expressing gratitude for

- _____
- _____
- _____

Three mini goals for making today great

- _____
- _____
- _____

My Todays Affirmations, I am

- _____
- _____

Three things that happened today for which I am grateful

- _____
- _____
- _____

How I might have advanced the quality of my day

- _____
- _____

"I enjoy the process of creating a healthy and fit body"

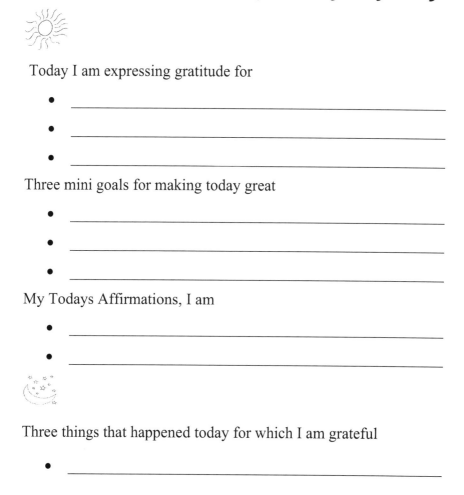

Today I am expressing gratitude for

- _____
- _____
- _____

Three mini goals for making today great

- _____
- _____
- _____

My Todays Affirmations, I am

- _____
- _____

Three things that happened today for which I am grateful

- _____
- _____
- _____

How I might have advanced the quality of my day

- _____
- _____

"I believe something wonderful is going to happen to me today"

Today I am expressing gratitude for

- _____
- _____
- _____

Three mini goals for making today great

- _____
- _____
- _____

My Todays Affirmations, I am

- _____
- _____

Three things that happened today for which I am grateful

- _____
- _____
- _____

How I might have advanced the quality of my day

- _____
- _____

"The universe is conspiring to make me feel happy and joyful"

Today I am expressing gratitude for

- _____
- _____
- _____

Three mini goals for making today great

- _____
- _____
- _____

My Todays Affirmations, I am

- _____
- _____

Three things that happened today for which I am grateful

- _____
- _____
- _____

How I might have advanced the quality of my day

- _____
- _____

"The more you help others, the more they will want to help you"

Today I am expressing gratitude for

- _____
- _____
- _____

Three mini goals for making today great

- _____
- _____
- _____

My Todays Affirmations, I am

- _____
- _____

Three things that happened today for which I am grateful

- _____
- _____
- _____

How I might have advanced the quality of my day

- _____
- _____

"The bridge between goals and success is discipline"

Today I am expressing gratitude for

- _____
- _____
- _____

Three mini goals for making today great

- _____
- _____
- _____

My Todays Affirmations, I am

- _____
- _____

Three things that happened today for which I am grateful

- _____
- _____
- _____

How I might have advanced the quality of my day

- _____
- _____

"If you are not moving towards your goals you are moving away from them"

Today I am expressing gratitude for

- _____
- _____
- _____

Three mini goals for making today great

- _____
- _____
- _____

My Todays Affirmations, I am

- _____
- _____

Three things that happened today for which I am grateful

- _____
- _____
- _____

How I might have advanced the quality of my day

- _____
- _____

"Successful people are simply those with success habits"

Today I am expressing gratitude for

- _____
- _____
- _____

Three mini goals for making today great

- _____
- _____
- _____

My Todays Affirmations, I am

- _____
- _____

Three things that happened today for which I am grateful

- _____
- _____
- _____

How I might have advanced the quality of my day

- _____
- _____

"See yourself living in abundance and you will attract it. It always works, it works every time with every person"

Today I am expressing gratitude for

- _____
- _____
- _____

Three mini goals for making today great

- _____
- _____
- _____

My Todays Affirmations, I am

- _____
- _____

Three things that happened today for which I am grateful

- _____
- _____
- _____

How I might have advanced the quality of my day

- _____
- _____

"No man can succeed in a line of endeavor which he does not like"

Today I am expressing gratitude for

- _____
- _____
- _____

Three mini goals for making today great

- _____
- _____
- _____

My Todays Affirmations, I am

- _____
- _____

Three things that happened today for which I am grateful

- _____
- _____
- _____

How I might have advanced the quality of my day

- _____
- _____

"Nature's plan to prepare you for great responsibilities is failure"

Today I am expressing gratitude for

- _____
- _____
- _____

Three mini goals for making today great

- _____
- _____
- _____

My Todays Affirmations, I am

- _____
- _____

Three things that happened today for which I am grateful

- _____
- _____
- _____

How I might have advanced the quality of my day

- _____
- _____

"Definiteness of purpose is the one quality that one must possess to win"

Today I am expressing gratitude for

- _____
- _____
- _____

Three mini goals for making today great

- _____
- _____
- _____

My Todays Affirmations, I am

- _____
- _____

Three things that happened today for which I am grateful

- _____
- _____
- _____

How I might have advanced the quality of my day

- _____
- _____

"The master key to your better future is you"

Today I am expressing gratitude for

- _____
- _____
- _____

Three mini goals for making today great

- _____
- _____
- _____

My Todays Affirmations, I am

- _____
- _____

Three things that happened today for which I am grateful

- _____
- _____
- _____

How I might have advanced the quality of my day

- _____
- _____

"A burning desire is the starting point of all success"

Today I am expressing gratitude for

- _____
- _____
- _____

Three mini goals for making today great

- _____
- _____
- _____

My Todays Affirmations, I am

- _____
- _____

Three things that happened today for which I am grateful

- _____
- _____
- _____

How I might have advanced the quality of my day

- _____
- _____

"There are no limitations to the mind except those we impose

Today I am expressing gratitude for

- _____
- _____
- _____

Three mini goals for making today great

- _____
- _____
- _____

My Todays Affirmations, I am

- _____
- _____

Three things that happened today for which I am grateful

- _____
- _____
- _____

How I might have advanced the quality of my day

- _____
- _____

"Success is walking from failure to failure with no loss of enthusiasm"

Today I am expressing gratitude for

- _____
- _____
- _____

Three mini goals for making today great

- _____
- _____
- _____

My Todays Affirmations, I am

- _____
- _____

Three things that happened today for which I am grateful

- _____
- _____
- _____

How I might have advanced the quality of my day

- _____
- _____

"The ladder of success is never crowded at the top"

Today I am expressing gratitude for

- _____
- _____
- _____

Three mini goals for making today great

- _____
- _____
- _____

My Todays Affirmations, I am

- _____
- _____

Three things that happened today for which I am grateful

- _____
- _____
- _____

How I might have advanced the quality of my day

- _____
- _____

"Don't wait the time will never be just right"

Today I am expressing gratitude for

- _____
- _____
- _____

Three mini goals for making today great

- _____
- _____
- _____

My Todays Affirmations, I am

- _____
- _____

Three things that happened today for which I am grateful

- _____
- _____
- _____

How I might have advanced the quality of my day

- _____
- _____

"Whatever the mind of a man can conceive and believe, it can achieve"

Today I am expressing gratitude for

- _____
- _____
- _____

Three mini goals for making today great

- _____
- _____
- _____

My Todays Affirmations, I am

- _____
- _____

Three things that happened today for which I am grateful

- _____
- _____
- _____

How I might have advanced the quality of my day

- _____
- _____

"Often opportunity comes disguised as a temporary defeat"

Today I am expressing gratitude for

- _____

- _____

- _____

Three mini goals for making today great

- _____

- _____

- _____

My Todays Affirmations, I am

- _____

- _____

Three things that happened today for which I am grateful

- _____

- _____

- _____

How I might have advanced the quality of my day

- _____

- _____

"Perspiration, persistence and patience make an unbeatable combination for success

Today I am expressing gratitude for

- _____
- _____
- _____

Three mini goals for making today great

- _____
- _____
- _____

My Todays Affirmations, I am

- _____
- _____

Three things that happened today for which I am grateful

- _____
- _____
- _____

How I might have advanced the quality of my day

- _____
- _____

"To earn more you must learn more"

Today I am expressing gratitude for

- _____
- _____
- _____

Three mini goals for making today great

- _____
- _____
- _____

My Todays Affirmations, I am

- _____
- _____

Three things that happened today for which I am grateful

- _____
- _____
- _____

How I might have advanced the quality of my day

- _____
- _____

Daily Affirmations

- I am worthy of a wealthy life.

- I deserve the gift of a great life.

- God's wealth is circulating in my life.

- Universe is abundant and there is an infinite source of supply.

- The more I receive the more I give, the more I give the more I receive.

- I am a Money Magnet.

- I have a Millionaire Mind.

- I am safe and life is abundant.

- What I choose to do today will shape today and create my tomorrow.

- The past does not equal to the future.

- Life is constantly happening for me.

- Healthy food is a gift and reward that I deserve every day.

- I control how I feel.

- Money comes to me in increasing quantity from multiple sources on a continuous basis.

Congratulations

You have successfully completed 90 days of Journaling, I am sure you must be experiencing positive changes in your life by now.

If you are experiencing benefits of this journal would you be kind enough to leave a review for this Journal on Amazon, that would be highly appreciated and we would be very grateful if in your review you can tell what changes are you experiencing in your lives as a result of Journaling.

Thank you very much for your purchase.

Printed in Great Britain
by Amazon